■SCHOLASTIC

10 Reading Comprehension Card Games

Reproducible, Easy-to-Play Card and Board Games That Boost Kids' Reading Skills — and Help Them Succeed on Tests

bright ideas™
from
Elaine Richard

NEW YORK • TORONTO • LONDON • AUCKLAND • SYDNEY
MEXICO CITY • NEW DELHI • HONG KONG • BUENOS AIRES

Teaching *Resources*

Dedication

These games are dedicated to:

all the children who worked with me over the
past 20 years to acquire good comprehension skills;

my three grandchildren—Katie, Sam, and Jake—
who played these games with me just for the fun of it;

the teachers, tutors, and parents dedicated to helping
every student achieve to the highest;

Andrea and Mark for their patient and indispensable computer tutoring;

and, of course, to Jack, for his patience, advice, and encouragement.

Cover and interior design by Holly Grundon
Illustrations by Kelly Kennedy

ISBN 0-439-62922-5
Copyright © 2005 by Elaine Richard
All rights reserved.
Printed in the U.S.A.

2 3 4 5 6 7 8 9 10   40   12 11 10 09 08 07 06 05

Contents

Introduction

Everyone agrees that the best way to build children's reading comprehension is to have them read, read, read. But that doesn't mean it's the only way. Enter *10 Reading Comprehension Card Games*! The games in this book help boost and reinforce essential reading skills—by giving students the kind of practice they'll enjoy doing over and over again.

As students play these super-fun games, they gain an understanding of main idea and plot, making inferences, sequencing, logical reasoning, drawing conclusions, cause and effect, and much more. Honing these skills leads to better comprehension, which is the cornerstone of successful reading, understanding, and studying skills.

Setting Up the Games

Most of the games require nothing more than the cards provided. Simply photocopy the game cards on cardstock, cut them apart, and store them in a plastic zipper bag along with a copy of the game instructions. Label the bag with the name of the game and store the bag in a filing box for easy access.

For a slightly more competitive twist, we also provide two generic game boards that can be used with any of the card games. Let students decide which game board to use for a particular game. (You might even invite students to create their own game boards.) Photocopy the game boards on regular copy paper then glue the pages to the inside of a manila folder, carefully aligning both sides of the game board. You could also photocopy the game board on cardstock and tape the two sides together. Consider laminating the game boards or covering them with clear plastic to keep them clean and sturdy for repeated use.

Playing the Games

The games in this book are designed for two to four players. A few can also be played at the board in a whole-class setting or in teams. You may want to establish some simple rules when you first introduce the games to avoid potential conflicts later on. For example, a quick solution to the question of who goes first is to have the youngest player always go first in a game, then play can move in a clockwise direction. A more traditional method would be to have players throw a number cube (or die) and the player with the highest number goes first. Then play continues in a clockwise direction.

Students might also play a game as "solitaire." In this case, the player writes the answers on a sheet of paper and hands it to you when he or she is finished. This could serve as an assessment tool to give you insight into the student's understanding.

Consider making the games part of the reading center or offering them as a choice during free time. You might also select a game to play with small reading groups, supervising the game to ensure appropriate answers. (Most of the games are open-ended and don't require exact answers. We provide possible answers for most games at the back of this book. You can photocopy the answer keys and give them to players to use for reference. Remind students that these are only possible answers. Accept any reasonable answers as long as players can justify them.)

Perhaps more effective than any of these options is to play the games in a one-on-one setting with an adult and a student, especially if the student needs extra help in any of the reading skills. A parent, teacher, or tutor can model more precise or interesting answers than peers might. Consider sending home copies of the games so students can play them with their families—another great way to strengthen the home–school connection.

However you decide to use the games in this book, they're sure to provide lots of fun and learning. Enjoy!

What's What?

> Given four words, players name the category in which they belong. In some cases, there may be more than one correct answer.

Objective

To help students understand main idea and generalization, and use expressive language to describe categories

Players

1 to 4 players (Single players can write their answers on a sheet of paper.)

You'll Need

- What's What? cards (pages 8–13)

Optional Materials

- Game board (choose one from pages 64–67)
- Game markers (buttons or coins work well)
- Number cube (die)

How to Play

1. Shuffle the "What's What?" cards and stack them facedown between the players.

2. Players take turns picking a card from the pile. On each turn, a player reads aloud the four words on the card and decides in which category the words belong. For example, if the words on the card are *desk*, *bed*, *chair*, *table*, a correct answer might be *furniture*.

3. If the player answers correctly, he keeps the card. If not, the next player can try to guess the answer. If she answers correctly, she keeps the card and takes another turn.

4. Continue taking turns until no cards are left. Players then count how many cards they've collected. The player with the most cards at the end of the game wins.

Playing With a Game Board

Each player places a marker on START. Play the game as described above. If a player answers correctly, he rolls the number cube to see how many spaces to move along the board. If the player doesn't answer correctly, he cannot move. Place used cards in a discard pile. The next player takes a turn. The first player to reach FINISH wins.

10 Reading Comprehension Card Games   Scholastic Teaching Resources

1

play   opera

ballet   concert

2

giggle   titter

roar   howl

3

storm   thunder

lightning   hail

4

music   static

chimes   drums

5

love   anger

joy   worry

6

violin   cello

bass   viola

7

peek   ogle

stare   glance

8

clock   sundial

hourglass   watch

9

What's What?

elbow   knee

hip   shoulder

13

What's What?

actor   professor

chemist   athlete

10

What's What?

dog   cat

canary   gerbil

14

What's What?

liter   pint

gallon   quart

11

What's What?

dictionary   thesaurus

encyclopedia   Internet

15

What's What?

ounce   pound

ton   gram

12

What's What?

teeth   palate

gums   tongue

16

What's What?

telephone   smoke signal

telegram   computer

17

What's What?

weak   frail

infirm   feeble

18

What's What?

tennis   badminton

volleyball   ping-pong

19

What's What?

ankle   arch

heel   toe

20

What's What?

grab   seize

snatch   hold

21

What's What?

ruler   pencils

desk   blackboard

22

What's What?

dough   eggs

milk   flour

23

What's What?

pail   mop

vacuum   broom

24

What's What?

soap   sink

towel   tub

25

What's What?

taste   see
smell   hear

26

What's What?

ball   mitt
bases   bat

27

What's What?

floor   ceiling
wall   door

28

What's What?

gloves   hat
scarf   boots

29

What's What?

bus   plane
boat   car

30

What's What?

sun   moon
lamp   candle

31

What's What?

zipper   snap
hook   button

32

What's What?

needle   thread
spool   pins

33

What's What?

runway   baggage
security   gate

34

What's What?

top   bottom
left   right

35

What's What?

jar   box
cage   vase

36

What's What?

back   front
right side   left side

37

What's What?

keys   lipstick
wallet   comb

38

What's What?

Army   Navy
Air Force   Coast Guard

39

What's What?

scream   shout
yell   holler

40

What's What?

veal   steak
chicken   pork chop

41

What's What?

tickets	screen
seats	popcorn

45

What's What?

pasta	pizza
scampi	scallopini

42

What's What?

brakes	steering wheel
seats	ignition

46

What's What?

fish	shells
seaweed	coral

43

What's What?

scissors	knife
saw	hatchet

47

What's What?

sunscreen	swimsuit
umbrella	blanket

44

What's What?

tacos	tortillas
burritos	fajitas

48

What's What?

scooter	bicycle
roller skates	tricycle

What's Not?

Players decide which word (out of four words) on a card does not belong and why.

Objective

To help students differentiate between like and unlike objects, and use expressive language to explain logic

Players

1 to 4 players (Single players can write their answers on a sheet of paper.)

You'll Need

- What's Not? cards (pages 15–20)

Optional Materials

- Game board (choose one from pages 64–67)
- Game markers (buttons or coins work well)
- Number cube (die)

How to Play

1. Shuffle the "What's Not?" cards and stack them facedown between the players.

2. Players take turns picking a card from the pile. On each turn, a player reads aloud the four words on the card and decides which three words belong together. She then explains why the fourth word doesn't belong. For example, if the words on the card are *pie, cookies, cake, ice cream*, a correct answer might be *ice cream* because even though all the words are desserts, ice cream is the only one that is not baked.

3. If the player answers correctly, she keeps the card. If not, the next player can try to guess the answer. If he answers correctly, he keeps the card and takes another turn.

4. Continue taking turns until no cards are left. Players then count how many cards they've collected. The player with the most cards at the end of the game wins.

Playing With a Game Board

Each player places a marker on START. Play the game as described above. If a player answers correctly, she rolls the number cube to see how many spaces to move along the board. If the player doesn't answer correctly, she cannot move. Place used cards in a discard pile. The next player takes a turn. The first player to reach FINISH wins.

10 Reading Comprehension Card Games   Scholastic Teaching Resources

1

What's Not?

west   east

south   both

2

What's Not?

copper   rubber

bronze   silver

3

What's Not?

ear   heel

ankle   knee

4

What's Not?

bee   butterfly

ant   hawk

5

What's Not?

towel   sheet

dress   notebook

6

What's Not?

chain   shoelace

ribbon   rope

7

What's Not?

concert   chorus

orchestra   jury

8

What's Not?

glass   water

window   mirror

9

What's Not?

bike   coffeemaker
blender   toaster

10

What's Not?

juice   soda
coffee   crayon

11

What's Not?

forty   sixth
tenth   fourth

12

What's Not?

harbor   bay
river   island

13

What's Not?

pen   book
newspaper   magazine

14

What's Not?

crayon   pencil
chalk   door

15

What's Not?

bat   mitt
sponge   ball

16

What's Not?

desk   table
bowl   bed

17

What's Not?

Mars	Earth
Venus	Metro

18

What's Not?

belt	bracelet
necklace	ring

19

What's Not?

flu	sprain
measles	chicken pox

20

What's Not?

peas	squash
bananas	carrots

21

What's Not?

Tuesday	Birthday
Wednesday	Saturday

22

What's Not?

bus	coat
car	airplane

23

What's Not?

yo-yo	doll
ball	green

24

What's Not?

dog	cat
squirrel	gerbil

25

What's Not?

elephant   canary

lion   tiger

26

What's Not?

hop   skip

clap   jump

27

What's Not?

raft   ferry

canoe   log

28

What's Not?

fork   hammer

wrench   screwdriver

29

What's Not?

brick   ice

popsicle   snowman

30

What's Not?

jar   funnel

vase   pitcher

31

What's Not?

ink   perfume

paint   pencil

32

What's Not?

veal   cheddar

steak   hamburger

33

What's Not?

person   group
club   team

34

What's Not?

circle   diamond
house   rectangle

35

What's Not?

cookies   soup
crackers   chips

36

What's Not?

sailor   artist
librarian   woman

37

What's Not?

fog   smile
tornado   sleet

38

What's Not?

spider   firefly
mosquito   crow

39

What's Not?

shoe   boat
life preserver   cork

40

What's Not?

brick   anchor
sponge   rock

41

What's Not?

tent   bicycle

helicopter   train

42

What's Not?

cake   decorations

candles   cottage

43

What's Not?

dishwasher   slide

seesaw   monkey bars

44

What's Not?

house   moon

ball   pearl

45

What's Not?

fish   whale

seaweed   cabin

46

What's Not?

fairy tales   fables

biographies   tall tales

47

What's Not?

hat   gloves

crown   helmet

48

What's Not?

daffodil   tulip

tree   orchid

Same/Different

> **Players decide how two words on a card are the same and/or different.**

Objective

To give students practice in comparing and contrasting two words

Players

2 to 4 players

You'll Need

- Same/Different cards (pages 22–25)
- Game board (choose one from pages 64–67)
- Game markers (buttons or coins)
- Same/Different cube* (right)

  * You can also write S, D, and S/D on small stickers
  and place them on a regular die.

← Fold on the solid lines.

How to Play

1. Shuffle the "Same/Different" cards and stack them facedown next to the game board. Each player places a marker on START.

2. On each turn, a player picks a card and rolls the cube. If the player rolls an "S" she explains how the two words on the card are alike. If she rolls a "D" she explains how the words are different. If she rolls an "S/D" she explains how the words are the same and different. For instance, say the words are *sun* and *lamp*. The words are the same in that they both give light. They are different in that one is in the sky and the other is in a house.

3. If the player had rolled an "S" or "D" and answers correctly, she may move the number of spaces written on the card. If she had rolled an "S/D" and answers correctly, she moves twice the number of spaces on the card. If the player doesn't answer correctly, she doesn't move. The next player takes a turn.

4. The first player to reach FINISH wins.

1   Same/Different

wool   satin

(2)

2   Same/Different

Sunday   January

(2)

3   Same/Different

excited   anxious

(3)

4   Same/Different

president   king

(2)

5   Same/Different

ankle   wrist

(1)

6   Same/Different

toy   game

(1)

7   Same/Different

hill   mountain

(1)

8   Same/Different

carrot   radish

(1)

9   Same/Different

cottage   mansion

(2)

10   Same/Different

sometimes   always

(2)

11   Same/Different

ladder   stairs

(1)

12   Same/Different

harbor   ocean

(1)

13 — Same/Different

brook   river
_____
(1)

19 — Same/Different

sundial   hourglass
_____
(2)

14 — Same/Different

smoke   steam
_____
(2)

20 — Same/Different

photograph   poster
_____
(2)

15 — Same/Different

basketball   soccer
_____
(1)

21 — Same/Different

collar   scarf
_____
(1)

16 — Same/Different

silent   calm
_____
(2)

22 — Same/Different

escalator   elevator
_____
(1)

17 — Same/Different

zookeeper   veterinarian
_____
(2)

23 — Same/Different

postcard   letter
_____
(1)

18 — Same/Different

waiter   chef
_____
(2)

24 — Same/Different

string beans   lettuce
_____
(2)

25 Same/Different

fence   wall

(2)

26 Same/Different

banana   peanut

(1)

27 Same/Different

bread   toast

(1)

28 Same/Different

generous   selfish

(3)

29 Same/Different

telephone   e-mail

(1)

30 Same/Different

guitar   cello

(2)

31 Same/Different

glue   nail

(1)

32 Same/Different

orchestra   band

(2)

33 Same/Different

skiing   ice-skating

(2)

34 Same/Different

box   bag

(1)

35 Same/Different

thermometer   speedometer

(2)

36 Same/Different

encyclopedia   dictionary

(1)

37   Same/Different

trumpet   violin
(2)

43   Same/Different

disappointment   excitement
(2)

38   Same/Different

smile   laugh
(2)

44   Same/Different

computer   brain
(2)

39   Same/Different

lawyer   judge
(3)

45   Same/Different

wonder   question
(3)

40   Same/Different

sip   gulp
(1)

46   Same/Different

canary   eagle
(2)

41   Same/Different

annoyed   angry
(2)

47   Same/Different

pancake   cupcake
(2)

42   Same/Different

boat   raft
(1)

48   Same/Different

vacation   recess
(1)

Cause or Effect?

> **Players decide which of two statements on each card is the cause and which is the effect.**

Objective

To develop logical reasoning, sequencing, and understanding of plot

Players

2 to 4 players

You'll Need

- Cause or Effect? cards (pages 27–30)

Optional Materials

- Game board (choose one from pages 64–67)
- Game markers (buttons or coins work well)
- Number cube (die)

How to Play

1. Shuffle the "Cause or Effect?" cards and stack them facedown between the players.

2. Players take turns picking a card from the pile. On each turn, a player reads the two statements on the card aloud. The player decides which statement is the cause and which is the effect. For example, say the card reads: *The lights went out. There was a power failure.* The second sentence is the cause and the first sentence is the effect. (HINT: If you can say *because* in front of one choice, that statement is the cause.)

3. If the player answers correctly, he keeps the card. If not, he puts the card in a discard pile. The next player takes a turn.

4. Continue taking turns until no cards are left. Players then count how many cards they've collected. The player with the most cards at the end of the game wins.

Playing With a Game Board

Each player places a marker on START. Play the game as described above. If a player answers correctly, he rolls the number cube to see how many spaces to move along the board. If the player doesn't answer correctly, he cannot move. Place used cards in a discard pile. The next player takes a turn. The first player to reach FINISH wins.

10 Reading Comprehension Card Games   Scholastic Teaching Resources

1	Cause or Effect?		7	Cause or Effect?
	achieve			illness
	try			virus

2	Cause or Effect?		8	Cause or Effect?
	destruction			celebration
	fire			anniversary

3	Cause or Effect?		9	Cause or Effect?
	teamwork			vote
	victory			election

4	Cause or Effect?		10	Cause or Effect?
	carelessness			good grades
	accident			studying

5	Cause or Effect?		11	Cause or Effect?
	flood			fireplace
	rain			warmth

6	Cause or Effect?		12	Cause or Effect?
	laughter			sunrise
	jokes			daylight

13 Cause or Effect?

We are late.

Let's take a taxi.

14 Cause or Effect?

We called the repairman.

The dishwasher broke.

15 Cause or Effect?

He hurt my feelings.

I felt angry.

16 Cause or Effect?

We felt tired but healthy.

We ran two miles.

17 Cause or Effect?

We were disappointed.

It rained at the picnic.

18 Cause or Effect?

The road was slippery.

Snow was turning to ice.

19 Cause or Effect?

Dinner got cold.

Our guests arrived late.

20 Cause or Effect?

I played tennis all day.

I was too tired to watch TV.

21 Cause or Effect?

It was cold outside.

I wore my jacket.

22 Cause or Effect?

Mother bought new crayons.

We drew pictures all day.

23 Cause or Effect?

We enjoyed the holiday.

Grandmother made a great turkey.

24 Cause or Effect?

He couldn't believe his luck.

He won first prize!

25 Cause or Effect?

I left my math book at school.

I couldn't do my homework.

31 Cause or Effect?

The milk spilled.

We mopped the floor.

26 Cause or Effect?

They were lost.

They asked the police for directions.

32 Cause or Effect?

We needed to find facts for our research paper.

We went to the library.

27 Cause or Effect?

The dog ate my book report.

I can't hand in my report.

33 Cause or Effect?

Everyone cheered.

The rocket was successfully launched.

28 Cause or Effect?

She had a stomachache.

She ate candy, popcorn, pizza, and soda.

34 Cause or Effect?

She looked ecstatic!

She rode her new two-wheeler for the first time.

29 Cause or Effect?

He wants to buy a present for his friend.

He's saving his allowance.

35 Cause or Effect?

There was an eclipse of the sun.

Everything became dark during the day.

30 Cause or Effect?

The elephants were on parade.

The circus is coming.

36 Cause or Effect?

Fred is the new boy in our class.

I'll try to make friends with Fred.

37 Cause or Effect?

The baby woke up and cried.

The telephone rang loudly.

---

38 Cause or Effect?

He got a suntan.

He spent the day at the beach.

---

39 Cause or Effect?

He was worried.

He hadn't studied for the test.

---

40 Cause or Effect?

She was excited!

Her uncle gave her a dog.

---

41 Cause or Effect?

We called the police.

There was an accident down the street.

---

42 Cause or Effect?

The storyline was really funny.

We enjoyed the movie.

---

43 Cause or Effect?

She's not my best friend anymore.

She tells all my secrets.

---

44 Cause or Effect?

I love the outdoors and sports.

I want to go to sleep-away camp next summer.

---

45 Cause or Effect?

I like to read before bedtime.

Reading is very relaxing.

---

46 Cause or Effect?

I want to go out for dinner on my birthday.

Restaurants make me feel grown-up.

---

47 Cause or Effect?

I came home late.

Mother was very worried.

---

48 Cause or Effect?

Popcorn is our favorite treat.

We bought popcorn at the movies.

Perplexed

Players try to name something that a card describes.

Objective

To broaden students' understanding of rich language and metaphor in reading; to encourage creative thinking that goes beyond the concrete; to enhance the use of more colorful language in speaking and writing

Players

1 or more players (Single players can write their answers on a sheet of paper. This game can also be played in a whole-class setting, with the teacher writing responses on the board.)

You'll Need

- Perplexed cards (pages 32–35)

Optional Materials

- Game board (choose one from pages 64–67)
- Game markers (buttons or coins work well)
- Number cube (die)

How to Play

1. Shuffle the "Perplexed" cards and stack them facedown between the players.

2. Players take turns picking a card from the pile. On each turn, a player reads the statement on the card aloud. The player tries to name what the statement describes.

3. If the player's answer makes sense, she keeps the card. If not, the next player can try to come up with a better answer. If he does, he keeps the card and takes another turn.

4. Continue taking turns until no cards are left. Players then count how many cards they've collected. The player with the most cards at the end of the game wins.

Playing With a Game Board

Each player places a marker on START. Play the game as described above. If a player answers correctly, she rolls the number cube to see how many spaces to move along the board. If the player doesn't answer correctly, she cannot move. Place used cards in a discard pile. The next player takes a turn. The first player to reach FINISH wins.

10 Reading Comprehension Card Games · Scholastic Teaching Resources

1 ◎ **Perplexed** ◎

Name something that ...
grows but does not get taller.

2 ◎ **Perplexed** ◎

Name something that ...
closes but does not lock.

3 ◎ **Perplexed** ◎

Name something that ...
flies but does not walk.

4 ◎ **Perplexed** ◎

Name something that ...
melts but is not frozen.

5 ◎ **Perplexed** ◎

Name something that ...
has bark but has no bite.

6 ◎ **Perplexed** ◎

Name something that ...
**smells good but would
not taste good.**

7 ◎ **Perplexed** ◎

Name something that ...
can be heard but cannot be seen.

8 ◎ **Perplexed** ◎

Name something that ...
is a liquid that you cannot drink.

9 ◎ **Perplexed** ◎

Name something that ...
is tough but not hard.

10 ◎ **Perplexed** ◎

Name something that ...
can be heard but not spoken.

11 ◎ **Perplexed** ◎

Name something that ...
floats but is not light.

12 ◎ **Perplexed** ◎

Name something that ...
is rough but not hard.

13 | Perplexed

Name something that ...
is long but not thin.

19 | Perplexed

Name something that ...
can be brushed but not combed.

14 | Perplexed

Name something that ...
breaks but is not glass.

20 | Perplexed

Name something that ...
can be felt but not seen.

15 | Perplexed

Name something that ...
bends but is not rubber.

21 | Perplexed

Name something that ...
is expensive but not big.

16 | Perplexed

Name something that ...
moves but is not alive.

22 | Perplexed

Name something that ...
can be seen but not touched.

17 | Perplexed

Name something that ...
can be caught but not thrown.

23 | Perplexed

Name something that ...
plays but does not have fun.

18 | Perplexed

Name something that ...
is round but does not roll.

24 | Perplexed

Name something that ...
runs but cannot walk.

25 Perplexed

Name something that …
is big but not heavy.

26 Perplexed

Name something that …
is heavy but not big.

27 Perplexed

Name something that …
is sharp but not pointed.

28 Perplexed

Name something that …
tastes sweet but is not sugar.

29 Perplexed

Name something that …
**has four suits but you wouldn't
hang them in a closet.**

30 Perplexed

Name something that …
whistles but is not a person.

31 Perplexed

Name something that …
**cannot count but makes
you a year older.**

32 Perplexed

Name something that …
has two hands but no feet.

33 Perplexed

Name something that …
has wrinkles but cannot be ironed.

34 Perplexed

Name something that …
hurts but does not bruise.

35 Perplexed

Name something that …
growls but is not an animal.

36 Perplexed

Name something that …
lights up but isn't a bulb.

37 **Perplexed**

Name something that ...
**is a horse you can ride
but can't feed.**

43 **Perplexed**

Name something that ...
**goes into your mouth
but is not swallowed.**

38 **Perplexed**

Name something that ...
is a bird but can't fly.

44 **Perplexed**

Name something that ...
has feet but no hands.

39 **Perplexed**

Name something that ...
**is time off from school
that isn't vacation.**

45 **Perplexed**

Name something that ...
has teeth but cannot bite.

40 **Perplexed**

Name something that ...
has waves but isn't the ocean.

46 **Perplexed**

Name something that ...
jumps but does not run.

41 **Perplexed**

Name something that ...
**is something you need to know
before you give the right answer.**

47 **Perplexed**

Name something that ...
**you play with but are not
friends with.**

42 **Perplexed**

Name something that ...
**can be jumbo or extra large but
whose name means "small."**

48 **Perplexed**

Name something that ...
grows down, not up.

Don't Mention It!

> Players take turns giving each other clues about the words or phrase on the card—without saying any of the words.

Objective

To give students practice in making inferences, drawing conclusions, and using expressive language

Players

2 to 4 players (best for two players)

You'll Need

- Don't Mention It! cards (pages 37–40)
- Game board (choose one from pages 64–67)
- Game markers (buttons or coins work well)

How to Play

1. Shuffle the "Don't Mention It!" cards and stack them facedown next to the game board. Players place their markers on START.

2. Players take turns being the "clue giver" and the "guesser." (If there are more than two players, the "guesser" is the person to the right of the "clue giver.") The "clue giver" picks up a card, reads it silently, and places it facedown on a discard pile. He then gives the "guesser" clues—without using the words on the card—to help her guess the word or phrase on the card. Clues may describe, give examples, and so on.

3. If the "guesser" guesses correctly, the "clue giver" moves the number of spaces written on the card. If not, the "clue giver" doesn't move and the next player takes a turn.

4. The first player to reach FINISH wins.

10 Reading Comprehension Card Games   Scholastic Teaching Resources

1 Don't Mention It!

Things that are sticky

(2)

2 Don't Mention It!

Things used for cooking

(1)

3 Don't Mention It!

Things that fly

(1)

4 Don't Mention It!

Things that make music

(1)

5 Don't Mention It!

Things you can eat raw

(2)

6 Don't Mention It!

Setting the table

(2)

7 Don't Mention It!

Grandparents

(2)

8 Don't Mention It!

A soccer game

(2)

9 Don't Mention It!

Things at an amusement park

(2)

10 Don't Mention It!

Things you must keep in
the refrigerator

(2)

11 Don't Mention It!

A movie theater

(3)

12 Don't Mention It!

Things that are baked

(2)

13 Don't Mention It!

Things at the beach

(2)

19 Don't Mention It!

Things that have sharp points

(3)

14 Don't Mention It!

Thanksgiving dinner

(1)

20 Don't Mention It!

Things you write with

(2)

15 Don't Mention It!

Things in the daytime sky

(2)

21 Don't Mention It!

Things you can win

(3)

16 Don't Mention It!

Noisy things

(2)

22 Don't Mention It!

Summer sports

(2)

17 Don't Mention It!

Things made of glass

(2)

23 Don't Mention It!

Things that are furry

(2)

18 Don't Mention It!

Things on a globe

(2)

24 Don't Mention It!

A classroom

(1)

25 Don't Mention It!

Things that can hang on the wall

(3)

31 Don't Mention It!

Things you need tickets for

(3)

26 Don't Mention It!

Things that you see in the city

(2)

32 Don't Mention It!

Things with a bell

(2)

27 Don't Mention It!

Things you can wear on your feet

(2)

33 Don't Mention It!

Melting ice cream

(2)

28 Don't Mention It!

Things that you see at a farm

(2)

34 Don't Mention It!

Apple pie à la mode

(3)

29 Don't Mention It!

Things people save

(3)

35 Don't Mention It!

Things on a bus

(2)

30 Don't Mention It!

A bicycle

(2)

36 Don't Mention It!

Food at a barbecue

(1)

37 Don't Mention It!

Things that have numbers on them

(3)

38 Don't Mention It!

Clothing you wouldn't wear outside the house

(3)

39 Don't Mention It!

Things at a party

(1)

40 Don't Mention It!

Supermarket jobs

(2)

41 Don't Mention It!

A catcher's mitt

(2)

42 Don't Mention It!

A birthday present

(1)

43 Don't Mention It!

A canoe

(2)

44 Don't Mention It!

A fence

(2)

45 Don't Mention It!

Computer keyboard

(2)

46 Don't Mention It!

Bacon and eggs

(2)

47 Don't Mention It!

Green vegetables

(2)

48 Don't Mention It!

Types of hats

(2)

Here's the Answer! (What's the Question?)

> **Players think of a question that is appropriate to the answer given on each card.**

Objective

To encourage plot development by giving students practice in making assumptions, creating situations, and describing solutions

Players

2 to 4 players

You'll Need

- Here's the Answer! cards (pages 42–45)

Optional Materials

- Game board (choose one from pages 64–67)
- Game markers (buttons or coins work well)
- Number cube (die)

How to Play

1. Shuffle the "Here's the Answer!" cards and stack them facedown between the players.

2. Players take turns picking a card from the pile. On each turn, a player reads the answer on the card aloud. She then thinks of a question that can be answered by the words on the card. For example, say the card reads: *A present.* An appropriate question could be: *What do you get on your birthday?*

3. If the others agree that the question is appropriate, the player can keep the card. If the others disagree, she puts the card in a discard pile. The next player takes a turn.

4. Continue taking turns until no cards are left. Players then count how many cards they've collected. The player with the most cards at the end of the game wins.

Playing With a Game Board

Each player places a marker on START. Play the game as described above. If a player answers correctly, she rolls the number cube to see how many spaces to move along the board. If the player doesn't answer correctly, she cannot move. Place used cards in a discard pile. The next player takes a turn. The first player to reach FINISH wins.

10 Reading Comprehension Card Games   Scholastic Teaching Resources

1 Here's the Answer!

To see better

2 Here's the Answer!

June, July, August

3 Here's the Answer!

At a picnic

4 Here's the Answer!

In the refrigerator

5 Here's the Answer!

At school

6 Here's the Answer!

A Frisbee™

7 Here's the Answer!

Because it is hot

8 Here's the Answer!

At a dock

9 Here's the Answer!

At dawn

10 Here's the Answer!

A thermos

11 Here's the Answer!

A lifeguard

12 Here's the Answer!

So it will melt

13 Here's the Answer!

A passenger

19 Here's the Answer!

Toothpaste

14 Here's the Answer!

She cried

20 Here's the Answer!

Every day

15 Here's the Answer!

An umpire

21 Here's the Answer!

To the zoo

16 Here's the Answer!

Grapes

22 Here's the Answer!

We cheered

17 Here's the Answer!

An usher

23 Here's the Answer!

Because they don't have wings

18 Here's the Answer!

A king

24 Here's the Answer!

The man in the moon

25 Here's the Answer!

Mustard and ketchup

31 Here's the Answer!

Peanut butter and jelly

26 Here's the Answer!

A detective

32 Here's the Answer!

Hot soup

27 Here's the Answer!

A bird

33 Here's the Answer!

We called a locksmith.

28 Here's the Answer!

At night

34 Here's the Answer!

We missed the bus.

29 Here's the Answer!

Because it's snowing

35 Here's the Answer!

A plumber

30 Here's the Answer!

Because it's raining

36 Here's the Answer!

An electrician

37 Here's the Answer!

A carpenter

38 Here's the Answer!

A pharmacist

39 Here's the Answer!

A tailor

40 Here's the Answer!

A pilot

41 Here's the Answer!

At a birthday party

42 Here's the Answer!

A calendar

43 Here's the Answer!

Markers

44 Here's the Answer!

An eraser

45 Here's the Answer!

We stopped at the gas station.

46 Here's the Answer!

I was so-o-o-o hungry.

47 Here's the Answer!

We planned a surprise.

48 Here's the Answer!

He had a bad cold.

Do They Mean the Same Thing?

> **Players decide whether or not the two sentences on a card have the same meaning, and why they think so.**

Objective

To increase accuracy and inference in reading comprehension

Players

1 to 4 players (Single players can write their answers on a sheet of paper.)

You'll Need

- Do They Mean the Same Thing? cards (pages 47–52)

How to Play

1. Shuffle the "Do They Mean the Same Thing?" cards and stack them facedown between the players.

2. Players take turns picking a card from the pile. On each turn, a player reads the two sentences on the card aloud. The player then decides whether or not the two sentences mean the same thing. For example, these two sentences mean the same:

   He finished in first place.

   He won the race.

   These next two sentences do NOT:

   Only he went to the dentist. (No one else went to the dentist.)

   He only went to the dentist. (He didn't go anywhere else.)

   (HINT: Watch out for placement of words—like *just*, *even*, and *only*—in a sentence.)

3. If the player answers correctly, he keeps the card. If not, he puts the card in a discard pile. The next player takes a turn.

4. Continue taking turns until no cards are left. Players then count how many cards they've collected. The player with the most cards at the end of the game wins.

10 Reading Comprehension Card Games   Scholastic Teaching Resources

1 Do They Mean the Same Thing?

Only Joe loves spinach.

Joe loves only spinach.

5 Do They Mean the Same Thing?

Tom found his glasses on his books.

On his books, Tom found his glasses.

2 Do They Mean the Same Thing?

Grandma just went to the movies.

Just grandma went to the movies.

6 Do They Mean the Same Thing?

Jim is slightly taller than Bobby.

Bobby is almost as tall as Jim.

3 Do They Mean the Same Thing?

Most people like potato chips as much as pretzels.

Pretzels are as popular as potato chips.

7 Do They Mean the Same Thing?

Mary just fell asleep at 10 P.M.

Just Mary fell asleep at 10 P.M.

4 Do They Mean the Same Thing?

Mrs. Brown just helped Trisha.

Just Mrs. Brown helped Trisha.

8 Do They Mean the Same Thing?

Even Sally likes bowling.

Sally even likes bowling.

9 Do They Mean the Same Thing?

Daniel turned nine years old yesterday.

Daniel celebrated his ninth birthday yesterday.

10 Do They Mean the Same Thing?

Hot dogs are the favorite food at ballparks.

Everyone buys hot dogs at ballparks.

11 Do They Mean the Same Thing?

The score was 21 to 7 in favor of the Giants.

The Giants were losing by 14 points.

12 Do They Mean the Same Thing?

The Knicks tied the score at the end of the second quarter.

The score was tied at halftime.

13 Do They Mean the Same Thing?

The new baby resembled her mother.

The new baby looked like her mother.

14 Do They Mean the Same Thing?

After his shower, Bill went directly to bed.

Bill took a shower right before going to bed.

15 Do They Mean the Same Thing?

Katie writes in her diary only on Saturdays.

Katie only writes in her diary on Saturdays.

16 Do They Mean the Same Thing?

When Sam is at bat, he usually gets a hit.

Sam gets a hit most of the time he's at bat.

17   Do They Mean the Same Thing?

Jake just came home for dinner.

Jake came home just for dinner.

---

18   Do They Mean the Same Thing?

A school break is coming up
in two weeks.

In two weeks we'll have
some time off from school.

---

19   Do They Mean the Same Thing?

Mom left a note saying
she'd be back soon.

Mom's note said
she wouldn't be long.

---

20   Do They Mean the Same Thing?

Most kids get to school by bus.

A few kids get to school by
walking, biking, or riding in a car.

---

21   Do They Mean the Same Thing?

We eat only healthy foods
for snack at home.

We don't eat junk food
for snack at home.

---

22   Do They Mean the Same Thing?

Although they are twins,
they look very different.

They are fraternal twins,
not identical.

---

23   Do They Mean the Same Thing?

Dad is enthusiastic about
softball games.

Dad gets excited at softball games.

---

24   Do They Mean the Same Thing?

All the biography books
are on the lowest shelf.

There are no biography books
on the upper shelves.

25 Do They Mean the Same Thing?

Dad's only brother is Uncle John.

Dad is Uncle John's only brother.

26 Do They Mean the Same Thing?

Michelle feels comfortable only when she's wearing pants.

When Michelle wears dresses, she feels uncomfortable.

27 Do They Mean the Same Thing?

Some people are afraid only of snakes.

Only some people are afraid of snakes.

28 Do They Mean the Same Thing?

If you leave ice cream out of the freezer, it will melt.

Melted ice cream has been left out of the freezer.

29 Do They Mean the Same Thing?

Keisha had so many books, she couldn't even carry her bag.

Keisha had so many books, even Dad couldn't carry her bag.

30 Do They Mean the Same Thing?

The ambulance sped to the hospital, sirens screaming.

Sirens blaring, the ambulance drove to the hospital.

31 Do They Mean the Same Thing?

Danny even read the newest Harry Potter book.

Even Danny read the newest Harry Potter book.

32 Do They Mean the Same Thing?

The cats drink only milk.

Only the cats drink milk.

33 Do They Mean the Same Thing?

> Just Amelia hugged her
> teddy bear.
>
> ---
>
> Amelia just hugged her
> teddy bear.

37 Do They Mean the Same Thing?

> Ken works in the garden
> only on weekends.
>
> ---
>
> Ken works only in the
> garden on weekends.

34 Do They Mean the Same Thing?

> We didn't have time to eat
> dinner before the show started.
>
> ---
>
> We couldn't eat earlier
> so we ate after the show.

38 Do They Mean the Same Thing?

> Even in the kitchen,
> Mark is a pro.
>
> ---
>
> Mark is a pro even
> in the kitchen.

35 Do They Mean the Same Thing?

> Jenny even stayed
> overnight after the party.
>
> ---
>
> Even Jenny stayed overnight
> after the party.

39 Do They Mean the Same Thing?

> Jane just keeps
> asking questions.
>
> ---
>
> Just Jane keeps
> asking questions.

36 Do They Mean the Same Thing?

> Just as I came in the door,
> the phone rang.
>
> ---
>
> The phone rang
> just as I came in the door.

40 Do They Mean the Same Thing?

> Jen's collection had the
> most stamps in it.
>
> ---
>
> Jen had the most stamps
> in her collection.

41 Do They Mean the Same Thing?

Andrea was the only one brave enough to jump into the deep end.

Only Andrea was brave enough to jump into the deep end.

45 Do They Mean the Same Thing?

Even my parents went on the Ferris wheel.

My parents even went on the Ferris wheel.

42 Do They Mean the Same Thing?

Susan didn't even want to see that movie.

Even Susan didn't want to see that movie.

46 Do They Mean the Same Thing?

Just for fun, let's play tag.

Let's play tag just for fun.

43 Do They Mean the Same Thing?

Jon won the spelling bee in his class.

Jon is the best speller in his class.

47 Do They Mean the Same Thing?

Andy only wanted to read about horses.

Andy wanted to read only about horses.

44 Do They Mean the Same Thing?

Mike loves to read, especially at bedtime.

Mike loves to read only at bedtime.

48 Do They Mean the Same Thing?

He doesn't think Kim took the toy.

He thinks Kim didn't take the toy.

Sometimes, Always, Never

Players decide if the sentence on a card is sometimes, always, or never true.

Objective

To help students discriminate between what is true, partially true, and false; to understand absurdities

Players

2 to 4 players

You'll Need

- Sometimes, Always, Never cards (pages 54–57)

Optional Materials

- Game board (choose one from pages 64–67)
- Game markers (buttons or coins work well)
- Number cube (die)

How to Play

1. Shuffle the "Sometimes, Always, Never" cards and stack them facedown between the players.

2. Players take turns picking a card from the pile. On each turn, a player reads the sentence on the card aloud. The player then says whether the sentence is true sometimes, all of the time, or never.

3. If the player answers correctly, he keeps the card. If not, he puts the card in a discard pile. The next player takes a turn.

4. Continue taking turns until no cards are left. Players then count how many cards they've collected. The player with the most cards at the end of the game wins.

Playing With a Game Board

Each player places a marker on START. Play the game as described above. If a player answers correctly, he rolls the number cube to see how many spaces to move along the board. If the player doesn't answer correctly, he cannot move. Place used cards in a discard pile. The next player takes a turn. The first player to reach FINISH wins.

10 Reading Comprehension Card Games   Scholastic Teaching Resources

1 Sometimes, Always, Never

Ferris wheels rotate.

2 Sometimes, Always, Never

It rains when it's cloudy.

3 Sometimes, Always, Never

People have freckles.

4 Sometimes, Always, Never

Keys open locks.

5 Sometimes, Always, Never

Shoes have zippers.

6 Sometimes, Always, Never

A suit comes with pants.

7 Sometimes, Always, Never

A waterfall has a rainbow.

8 Sometimes, Always, Never

Mothers are women.

9 Sometimes, Always, Never

Women are mothers.

10 Sometimes, Always, Never

A dictionary has definitions.

11 Sometimes, Always, Never

Apples are sweet and red.

12 Sometimes, Always, Never

Bottles are made of wool.

13 Sometimes, Always, Never

Ice skates have wheels.

14 Sometimes, Always, Never

Limbs grow out of trees.

15 Sometimes, Always, Never

A TV set has a picture tube.

16 Sometimes, Always, Never

A telephone has
a busy signal.

17 Sometimes, Always, Never

Fish live underwater.

18 Sometimes, Always, Never

Sandwiches are on bread.

19 Sometimes, Always, Never

Trains run on tracks.

20 Sometimes, Always, Never

Neighbors are friendly.

21 Sometimes, Always, Never

Kindergarten has children.

22 Sometimes, Always, Never

Athletes like competition.

23 Sometimes, Always, Never

Arithmetic uses numbers.

24 Sometimes, Always, Never

Schools are closed
on Mondays.

25 Sometimes, Always, Never

Clocks have numbers.

31 Sometimes, Always, Never

Brothers are boys.

26 Sometimes, Always, Never

You wear socks over boots.

32 Sometimes, Always, Never

You can see the sun
in the daytime.

27 Sometimes, Always, Never

You put on your coat
before your shirt.

33 Sometimes, Always, Never

A sweater goes on
over your head.

28 Sometimes, Always, Never

Cousins are relatives.

34 Sometimes, Always, Never

The army has sailors.

29 Sometimes, Always, Never

Grouches are happy.

35 Sometimes, Always, Never

You can play ball
on the beach.

30 Sometimes, Always, Never

Girls have brothers.

36 Sometimes, Always, Never

Girls jump rope.

37 Sometimes, Always, Never

Maps show you where countries are.

38 Sometimes, Always, Never

The moon cannot be seen during the day.

39 Sometimes, Always, Never

You can learn things from TV.

40 Sometimes, Always, Never

Pasta has sauce on it.

41 Sometimes, Always, Never

Chocolate tastes sour.

42 Sometimes, Always, Never

Fourth graders drive cars.

43 Sometimes, Always, Never

Trains are faster than jet planes.

44 Sometimes, Always, Never

Toy bears can attack people.

45 Sometimes, Always, Never

A broken vase looks the same when mended.

46 Sometimes, Always, Never

Eggs are perfectly round.

47 Sometimes, Always, Never

An elephant is faster than a horse.

48 Sometimes, Always, Never

Calendars tell the time of day.

Stop the Flood!

> **Players read aloud the word on a card quickly and accurately.**

Objective

To help students develop automaticity in reading single words (without the help of context clues) easily and smoothly

Players

2 players, or 2 teams of 2 players each

Materials

- Stop the Flood! cards (pages 59–61)
- Game board (pages 62–63)

How to Play

1. Shuffle the "Stop the Flood!" cards and stack them facedown next to the game board. Each player picks a side of the game board.

2. On each turn, a player picks a card and immediately reads the word aloud.

3. If the player reads the word correctly, he puts the card (boulder) on his side of the game board (dam) to prevent the FLOOD. If he reads the word incorrectly, he returns the card anywhere in the stack.

   If the player picks a card with a letter on it, he must place the card on the corresponding letter on his side of the board. If he picks a letter card and that letter is already covered on his side of the board, he can return the card anywhere in the stack. The next player takes a turn.

4. Players continue taking turns reading the cards and placing them on the dam. The player who fills up all the boulders on his side of the board before placing the last letter of "FLOOD" wins.

Stop the Flood!	Stop the Flood!	Stop the Flood!
answer	when	though
Stop the Flood!	Stop the Flood!	Stop the Flood!
around	where	which
Stop the Flood!	Stop the Flood!	Stop the Flood!
every	bread	witch
Stop the Flood!	Stop the Flood!	Stop the Flood!
even	beard	does
Stop the Flood!	Stop the Flood!	Stop the Flood!
enough	board	goes
Stop the Flood!	Stop the Flood!	Stop the Flood!
ever	broad	already

Stop the Flood!	Stop the Flood!	Stop the Flood!
again	thought	believe
Stop the Flood!	**Stop the Flood!**	**Stop the Flood!**
there	rough	earthly
Stop the Flood!	**Stop the Flood!**	**Stop the Flood!**
three	caught	early
Stop the Flood!	**Stop the Flood!**	**Stop the Flood!**
their	cough	however
Stop the Flood!	**Stop the Flood!**	**Stop the Flood!**
doesn't	no one	shouldn't
Stop the Flood!	**Stop the Flood!**	**Stop the Flood!**
together	because	wouldn't

Stop the Flood!

someone

Stop the Flood!

everywhere

Stop the Flood!

D

Stop the Flood!

couldn't

Stop the Flood!

thorough

Stop the Flood!

F

Stop the Flood!

guest

Stop the Flood!

F

Stop the Flood!

L

Stop the Flood!

guess

Stop the Flood!

L

Stop the Flood!

O

Stop the Flood!

taught

Stop the Flood!

O

Stop the Flood!

O

Stop the Flood!

nowhere

Stop the Flood!

O

Stop the Flood!

D

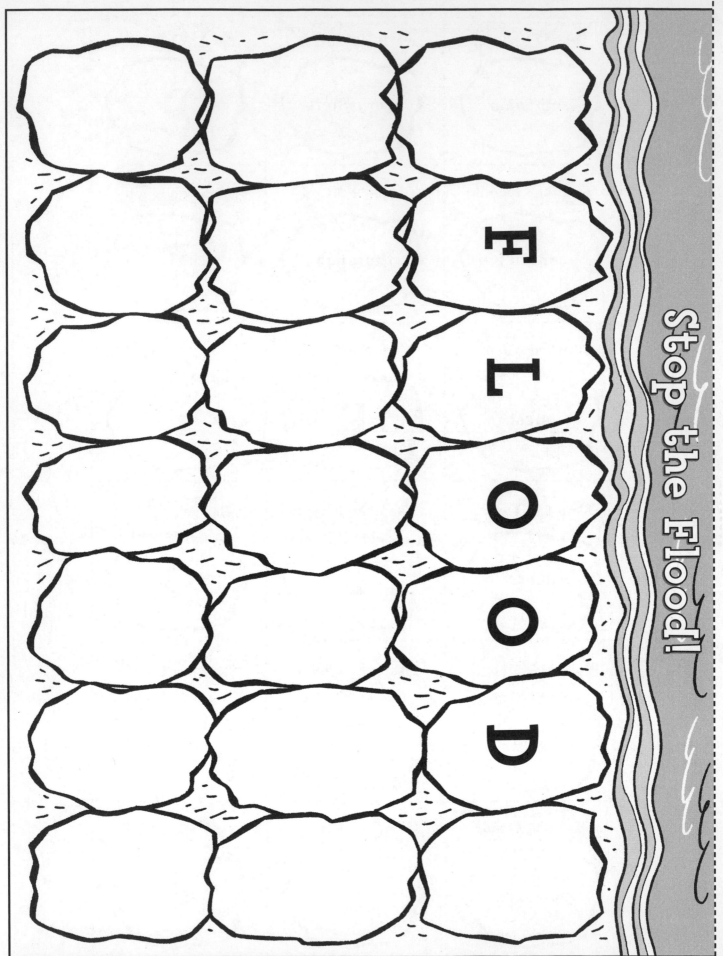

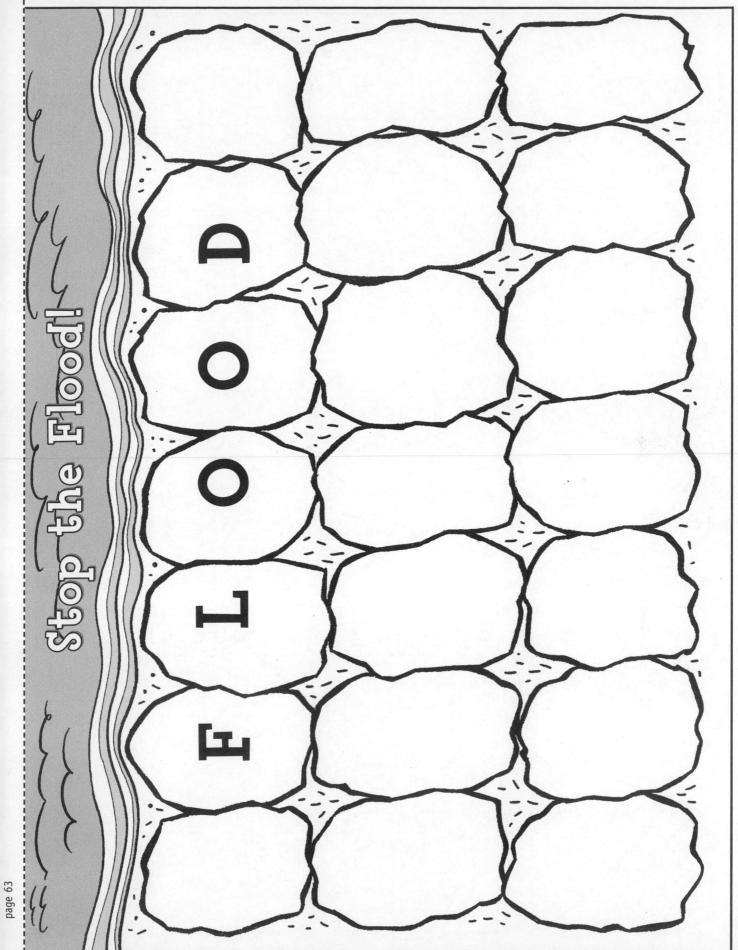

Stop the Flood!

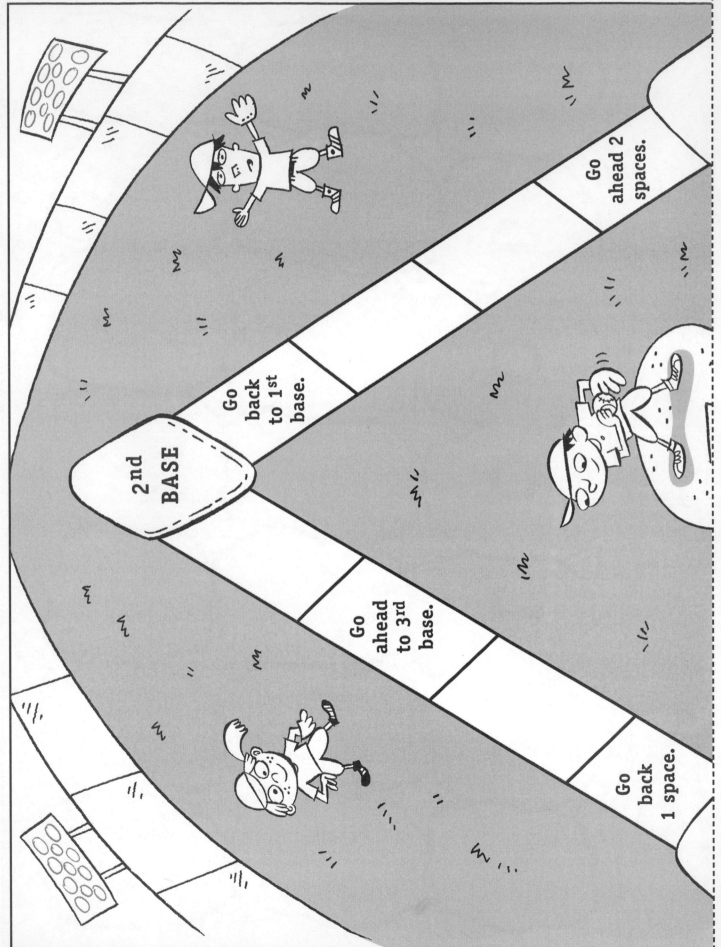

1st BASE

Go back 1 space.

HOME PLATE (Start/Finish)

Go back to 2nd base.

Go ahead 1 space.

3rd BASE

Lose a turn.

Take another turn.

Go ahead 2 spaces.

Go back 4 spaces.

Go back 1 space.

Go back 3 spaces.

START

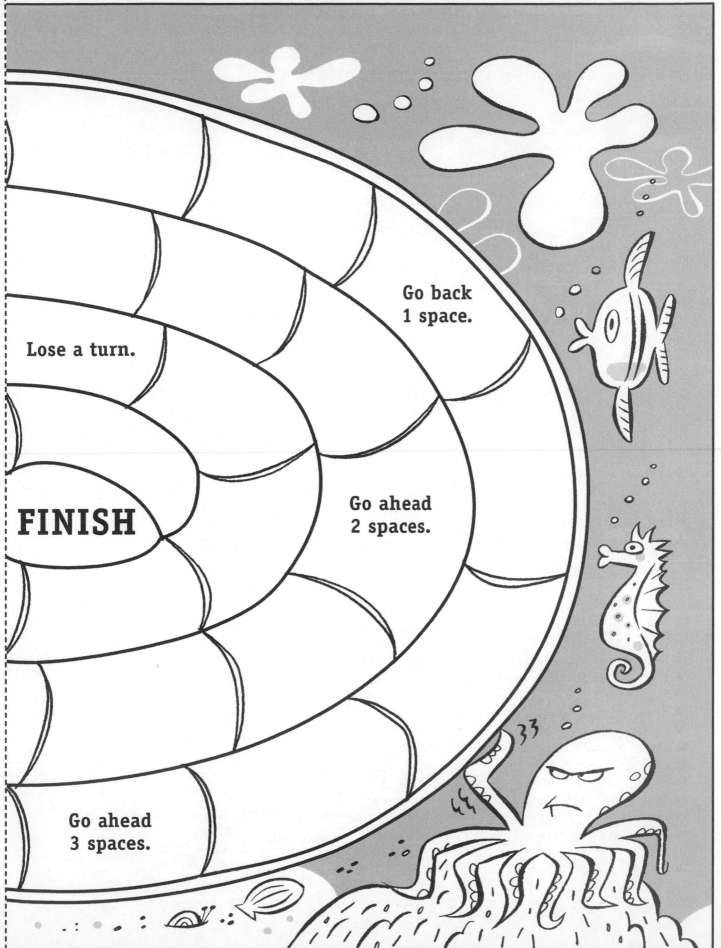

Go back
1 space.

Lose a turn.

Go ahead
2 spaces.

FINISH

Go ahead
3 spaces.

Possible Answers **What's What?** (page 7)

1. Performing arts
2. Synonyms for *laugh*
3. Weather
4. Sound
5. Emotions
6. Musical instruments
7. Synonyms for *look*
8. Things that tell time
9. Parts of the body
10. Pets
11. Resources (for research)
12. Parts of the mouth
13. Professions or jobs
14. Liquid measurements
15. Weights
16. Modes of communication
17. Antonyms of *strong*
18. Ball games
19. Parts of the foot
20. What hands do
21. Things in a classroom
22. Baking ingredients
23. Things for cleaning
24. Things in a bathroom
25. Senses
26. Baseball
27. Parts of a house or room
28. Winter wear
29. Modes of transportation
30. Things that give light
31. Clothes fasteners
32. Sewing materials
33. Airport
34. Direction words
35. Containers
36. Sides or directions
37. Things in a woman's purse
38. Military
39. Synonyms for *speak loudly*
40. Meat
41. Movie theater
42. Parts of a car
43. Sharp tools
44. Mexican foods
45. Italian foods
46. Things in the ocean
47. Things to bring to the beach
48. Things on wheels

Possible Answers **What's Not?** (page 14)

1. Both; not a compass direction
2. Rubber; not a metal
3. Ear; not a part of the leg
4. Hawk; not an insect
5. Notebook; not made of cloth
6. Chain; not something you can tie
7. Jury; not related to music
8. Water; not made of glass
9. Bike; not a kitchen appliance
10. Crayon; not something to drink
11. Forty; not an ordinal number
12. Island; not a body of water
13. Pen; not something you read
14. Door; not something you write with
15. Sponge; not something you use to play baseball
16. Bowl; not furniture
17. Metro; not a planet
18. Belt; not jewelry
19. Sprain; not a disease
20. Bananas; not vegetables
21. Birthday; not a day of the week
22. Coat; not transportation
23. Green; not a toy
24. Squirrel; not a pet
25. Canary; not a wild animal
26. Clap; not moving with legs
27. Log; not a type of boat
28. Fork; not a construction tool
29. Brick; not frozen
30. Funnel; does not hold water
31. Perfume; not something you use with paper
32. Cheddar; not meat
33. Person; not a collection of people
34. House; not a shape
35. Soup; not a crunchy snack
36. Woman; not a profession
37. Smile; not a weather phenomenon
38. Spider; does not fly
39. Shoe; does not float
40. Sponge; does not sink
41. Tent; not transportation
42. Cottage; not related to birthday
43. Dishwasher; not playground equipment
44. House; not round
45. Cabin; not found in the ocean
46. Biographies; not fiction
47. Gloves; not something you'd wear on your head
48. Tree; not a flower

Same/Different (page 21)

1. S—they are types of cloth; D—wool is rough, satin is smooth

2. S—they are in a calendar; D—Sunday is a day of the week, January is a month

3. S—they are emotions; D—excited is generally a positive emotion, anxious is usually negative

4. S—they are heads of countries; D—a president is elected by people, a king inherits the throne

5. S—they are joints in the body; D—ankle is in the foot, wrist is in the hand

6. S—they are related to play; D—a toy is a thing you play with, a game doesn't have to be a thing

7. S—they are landforms; D—a hill is much lower than a mountain

8. S—they are root vegetables; D—a carrot is sweet, a radish is tangy

9. S—they are houses; D—a cottage is smaller, less luxurious than a mansion

10. S—they say how often something happens; D—sometimes doesn't happen all the time, unlike always

11. S—they are something you would climb; D—a ladder has rungs, stairs have steps

12. S—they are bodies of water; D—a harbor is much smaller than an ocean

13. S—they are bodies of water; D—a brook is smaller than a river

14. S—they are gaseous; D—smoke comes from fire, steam comes from heated water

15. S—they are ball games; D—basketball is played with the hands, soccer is played with the feet and head

16. S—they can mean quiet; D—silent is related to lack of sound, calm is related to feeling

17. S—they work with animals; D—a zookeeper takes care of animals in a zoo, a veterinarian is an animal doctor

18. S—they work in a restaurant; D—a waiter serves food, a chef cooks the food

19. S—they tell time; D—a sundial uses the sun and shadows, an hourglass uses sand

20. S—they show pictures; D—a photograph is taken by a camera, a poster is usually a large picture you hang on a wall

21. S—they cover the neck; D—a collar is part of a shirt, a scarf is something you wrap around your neck

22. S—they transport people up and down; D—an escalator is like moving stairs, an elevator is like a moving box or room

23. S—they are used for correspondence; D—a postcard has a picture on one side and can be used for short notes, while a letter can be longer

24. S—they are vegetables; D—string beans are like long pods, lettuce are leaves

25. S—they are barriers; D—a fence surrounds property, a wall helps hold up a house

26. S—they can be snacks; D—banana is soft, peanut is crunchy

27. S—they are used for sandwiches; D—bread is soft, toast is crunchy bread

28. S—they are characteristics of people; D—generous is a positive trait where a person is kind and openhanded, while selfish is a negative trait where a person thinks only of him- or herself

29. S—they are ways to communicate; D—people speak on the telephone and write when they use e-mail

30. S—they are stringed instruments; D—a guitar is played with fingers and sometimes a pick, a cello is played both with fingers and a bow

31. S—they are used to fasten things; D—glue is used mostly on paper, a nail is used on wood

32. S—they have people playing musical instruments; D—an orchestra is generally bigger than a band

33. S—they are winter sports; D—skiing is done on a snow-covered mountain, ice-skating is on a frozen pond or ice rink

34. S—they are containers; D—a box is firm and generally keeps its shape, a bag is generally soft and can take the shape of what's inside

35. S—they are measuring instruments; D—a thermometer measures temperature, a speedometer measures speed

36. S—they are reference books; D—an encyclopedia gives more details about something, a dictionary gives definitions

37. S—they are musical instruments; D—a trumpet is a wind instrument, a violin is a string instrument

38. S—they express happiness; D—a smile is quiet, a laugh is louder

39. S—they work in a courtroom; D—a lawyer either defends or prosecutes a person, a judge decides questions brought into a court of law

40. S—they describe how a liquid is swallowed; D—to sip is to drink a little at a time, to gulp is to drink a large amount at once

41. S—they describe negative feelings; D—annoyed is bothered or irritated by something, angry is a much stronger feeling than annoyed

42. S—they are water transportation; D—a boat generally has sides that come up from the bottom, a raft is completely flat

43. S—they are emotions; D—disappointment is something you feel when you don't get what you want, excitement is something you feel when you're expecting something good

44. S—they process information; D—a computer is made by humans, the brain is inside humans

45. S—they relate to thinking about or getting information about something; D—to wonder is to be curious about something, to question is to ask about something

46. S—they are birds; D—a canary is a tame and small bird, an eagle is a wild, large bird

47. S—they are types of food; D—a pancake is usually eaten for breakfast, a cupcake is usually eaten for a snack

48. S—they are breaks; D—vacation usually takes several days, recess takes several minutes

Cause or Effect? (page 26)

1. C–try; E–achieve
2. C–fire; E–destruction
3. C–teamwork; E–victory
4. C–carelessness; E–accident
5. C–rain; E–flood
6. C–jokes; E–laughter
7. C–virus; E–illness
8. C–anniversary; E–celebration
9. C–election; E–vote
10. C–studying; E–good grades
11. C–fireplace; E–warmth
12. C–sunrise; E–daylight
13. C–We are late.
    E–Let's take a taxi.
14. C–The dishwasher broke.
    E–We called the repairman.
15. C–He hurt my feelings.
    E–I felt angry.
16. C–We ran two miles.
    E–We felt tired but healthy.
17. C–It rained at the picnic.
    E–We were disappointed.
18. C–Snow was turning to ice.
    E–The road was slippery.
19. C–Our guests arrived late.
    E–Dinner got cold.

20. C–I played tennis all day.
    E–I was too tired to watch TV.
21. C–It was cold outside.
    E–I wore my jacket.
22. C–Mother bought new crayons.
    E–We drew pictures all day.
23. C–Grandmother made a great turkey.
    E–We enjoyed the holiday.
24. C–He won first prize!
    E–He couldn't believe his luck.
25. C–I left my math book at school.
    E–I couldn't do my homework.
26. C–They were lost.
    E–They asked the police for directions.
27. C–The dog ate my book report.
    E–I can't hand in my report.
28. C–She ate candy, popcorn, pizza, and soda.
    E–She had a stomachache.
29. C–He wants to buy a present for his friend.
    E–He's saving his allowance.
30. C–The circus is coming.
    E–The elephants were on parade.

31. C–The milk spilled.
    E–We mopped the floor.
32. C–We needed to find facts for our research paper.
    E–We went to the library.
33. C–The rocket was successfully launched.
    E–Everyone cheered.
34. C–She rode her new two-wheeler for the first time.
    E–She looked ecstatic!
35. C–There was an eclipse of the sun.
    E–Everything became dark during the day.
36. C–Fred is the new boy in our class.
    E–I'll try to make friends with Fred.
37. C–The telephone rang loudly.
    E–The baby woke up and cried.
38. C–He spent the day at the beach.
    E–He got a suntan.
39. C–He hadn't studied for the test.
    E–He was worried.

40. C–Her uncle gave her a dog.
    E–She was excited!
41. C–There was an accident down the street.
    E–We called the police.
42. C–The storyline was really funny.
    E–We enjoyed the movie.
43. C–She tells all my secrets.
    E–She's not my best friend anymore.
44. C–I love the outdoors and sports.
    E–I want to go to sleep-away camp next summer.
45. C–Reading is very relaxing.
    E–I like to read before bedtime.
46. C–Restaurants make me feel grown-up.
    E–I want to go out for dinner on my birthday.
47. C–I came home late.
    E–Mother was very worried.
48. C–Popcorn is our favorite treat.
    E–We bought popcorn at the movies.

Perplexed (page 31)

1. hair, nails, friendship
2. book, envelope, a play
3. airplane, kite, balloon
4. candle, butter
5. tree
6. perfume, flower
7. wind, echo, sound
8. gasoline, perfume
9. meat, rubber
10. chimes, wind, thunder
11. ship, coconut
12. sandpaper, Velcro
13. highway, time

14. computer, car
15. river, reed, road
16. wind-up toy, car
17. a cold
18. moon, sun
19. teeth
20. air, wind
21. diamond ring, cell phone
22. sun, cloud
23. tape recorder, radio
24. machine, engine
25. large balloon

26. brick
27. cheddar cheese, musical note, wit
28. honey, syrup
29. deck of cards
30. train, tea kettle
31. birthday
32. clock, watch
33. face
34. headache, stomachache, feelings
35. stomach
36. candle

37. sawhorse, rocking horse
38. ostrich, penguin
39. recess, weekends
40. hair, sound
41. question
42. shrimp
43. bubble gum, thermometer
44. yardstick
45. comb
46. kangaroo, frog
47. video games, toys
48. plant roots

Don't Mention It! (page 36)

Possible Answers

1. gum, glue, paste
2. frying pan, pot, pan
3. bird, bee, butterfly
4. piano, CD, singer
5. carrot, banana, celery
6. placemats, plates, forks, knives
7. Mom or Dad's mother and father
8. goalie, ball, no hands
9. roller coaster, Ferris wheel, merry-go-round
10. milk, eggs, yogurt
11. screen, popcorn, film, marquis
12. bread, cake, cookies, pie
13. sand, seashells, ocean, starfish
14. turkey, yams, mashed potatoes, sweet potato pie
15. sun, clouds
16. rattle, whistle, telephone, car horns
17. window, bottle
18. countries, oceans, compass rose
19. needles, pins, nails
20. pen, pencil, marker
21. a game, lottery, medal
22. baseball, volleyball, swimming
23. bear, squirrel, cat
24. tables, chairs, blackboard, teacher
25. paintings, pictures
26. tall buildings, buses, taxis, theaters
27. shoes, sandals, socks
28. barn, cows, chickens, hay, apple trees
29. money, souvenirs
30. something you ride with two wheels
31. movies, amusement-park rides, plays, sporting events
32. bicycle, trolley, church
33. favorite frozen treat that's been left out in the sun
34. favorite baked dessert with fruit inside and served with a scoop of ice cream
35. driver, passengers, seats
36. hamburgers, hot dogs, ribs, chicken
37. clock, telephone, calendar, calculator
38. bathrobe, pajamas
39. pointy hats, balloons, confetti, streamers
40. cashier, delivery person, stockperson, butcher
41. for catching baseball, especially behind home plate
42. something you get on a special once-a-year occasion
43. dugout boat, especially used by Native Americans
44. something that separates your yard from your neighbor's yard
45. something you type on, especially to do homework or surf the Internet
46. two things you eat for breakfast
47. lettuce, peas, broccoli
48. baseball cap, beret, fez, fedora

Here's the Answer! (page 41)

Possible Answers

1. Why might you wear eyeglasses?
2. What are the summer months?
3. Where would you eat sandwiches while sitting on a blanket at the park?
4. Where would you put milk or eggs so they wouldn't spoil?
5. Where do you learn reading, math, and science?
6. What do you call a round disc that you can throw back and forth with friends?
7. Why did you turn on the air conditioner?
8. Where would you "park" a boat?
9. When do roosters crow?
10. Where would you keep soup to keep it hot for lunch?
11. What do you call the person who makes sure people are safe in a swimming pool?
12. Why would you leave an ice cube under the hot sun?
13. What do you call a person who rides on a bus or taxicab?
14. What did she do when she fell and got hurt?
15. What do you call the person who calls balls and strikes in a baseball game?
16. What kind of fruit grows in bunches?
17. What do you call the person who shows or takes you to your seat in a theater?
18. Who is the head of a kingdom?
19. What do you put on your toothbrush to clean your teeth?
20. How often do you sleep?
21. Where can you go to see lions, tigers, bears, and other wild animals?
22. What did we do when our team scored?
23. Why can't pigs fly?
24. What do you call the "face" on a full moon?
25. What condiments do you put on hot dogs or hamburgers?
26. What do you call a person who looks for clues to solve mysteries?
27. What flies and lives in a nest?
28. When do you go to sleep?
29. Why are the kids planning to build a snowman?
30. Why are you wearing galoshes and carrying an umbrella?
31. What type of sandwich do most kids like?
32. What liquid can warm you up on a cold day?
33. What happened when we locked ourselves out of the house?
34. What happened when we arrived at the bus stop too late?
35. Who fixes leaks?
36. Who can help fix electrical wiring?
37. Who builds houses or makes furniture?
38. Who works in a drug store?
39. Who can fix clothes?
40. Who flies an airplane?
41. Where do you go to celebrate and bring a present to someone who just turned a year older?
42. What has dates on it?
43. What do you use to write on chart paper?
44. What do you use when you want to remove mistakes on your paper?
45. What happened when we found out that the gas tank was almost empty?
46. Why did I gulp down all my food really quickly?
47. What did we do when we wanted to have a party for someone without him knowing about it?
48. Why couldn't he come to school today?

Do They Mean the Same Thing? (page 46)

1. Not the same. The first sentence means Joe is the only one who loves spinach, while the second sentence means Joe doesn't love anything else but spinach.

2. Not the same. The first sentence means Grandma went to the movies a little while ago, while the second sentence means Grandma was the only one who went to the movies.

3. Same

4. Not the same. The first sentence means Mrs. Brown didn't help anyone else, while the second sentence means only Mrs. Brown helped Trisha.

5, 6. Same

7. Not the same. The first sentence means Mary fell asleep a short time ago, while the second sentence means Mary was the only one to fall asleep at 10 P.M.

8. Not the same. The first sentence means everyone including Sally likes bowling, while the second sentence could mean Sally likes many things including bowling.

9. Same

10. Not the same. Just because hot dogs are the favorite food at ballparks doesn't mean that everyone buys hot dogs at ballparks.

11. Not the same. The first sentence means that the Giants are leading the game, while the second sentence means the Giants are losing.

12, 13, 14. Same

15. Not the same. The first sentence means Katie doesn't write in her diary on any other day but Saturday, while the second sentence means Katie doesn't do anything but write in her diary on Saturdays.

16. Same

17. Not the same. The first sentence means Jake came home just a short time ago for dinner, while the second sentence means Jake came home only to eat dinner.

18, 19, 20, 21, 22, 23, 24, 25, 26. Same

27. Not the same. The first sentence means that some people are not afraid of anything other than snakes, while the second sentence means that not all people are afraid of snakes.

28. Same

29. Not the same. The first sentence says that Keisha can't carry her own bag, while the second sentence says that even Dad can't carry Keisha's bag.

30. Not the same. The first sentence says the ambulance was speeding, while the second sentence could mean that the ambulance was driving at normal speeds.

31. Not the same. The first sentence implies that Danny reads a lot of books including the newest Harry Potter book, while the second sentence implies that other people including Danny have read the newest book.

32. Not the same. The first sentence means the cats don't drink anything except milk, while the second sentence means that no one other than the cats drink milk.

33. Not the same. The first sentence means that no one else but Amelia hugged her teddy bear, while the second sentence means that Amelia hugged her teddy bear a few minutes ago, or that she didn't hug any other toys.

34. Same

35. Not the same. The first sentence means that Jenny not only came to the party but stayed over, while the second sentence means that Jenny and others stayed overnight after the party.

36. Same

37. Not the same. The first sentence means that Ken doesn't work in the garden except on weekends, while the second sentence means that Ken doesn't do any other work except gardening on weekends.

38. Same

39. Not the same. The first sentence means that Jane keeps on asking questions, while the second sentence means that no one except Jane asks questions.

40, 41. Same

42. Not the same. The first sentence means that Susan didn't want to do several things including see the movie, while the second sentence means that several people, including Susan, didn't want to see the movie.

43. Same

44. Not the same. The first sentence implies that Mike loves to read anytime but especially at bedtime, while the second sentence says that the only time Mike loves to read is at bedtime.

45. Not the same. The first sentence means that several people including my parents went on the Ferris wheel, while the second sentence means that my parents went on many rides including the Ferris wheel.

46, 47, 48. Same

Sometimes, Always, Never? (page 53)

1. Sometimes
2. Sometimes
3. Sometimes
4. Sometimes
5. Sometimes
6. Sometimes
7. Sometimes
8. Always
9. Sometimes
10. Always
11. Sometimes
12. Never
13. Never
14. Sometimes
15. Sometimes
16. Sometimes
17. Always
18. Always
19. Always
20. Sometimes
21. Always
22. Sometimes
23. Always
24. Sometimes
25. Sometimes
26. Never
27. Never
28. Always
29. Never
30. Sometimes
31. Always
32. Sometimes
33. Sometimes
34. Never
35. Sometimes
36. Sometimes
37. Sometimes
38. Sometimes
39. Sometimes
40. Sometimes
41. Never
42. Never
43. Never
44. Never
45. Sometimes
46. Sometimes
47. Never
48. Never